INCREDIBLE HOCKEY SHORT STORIES FOR KIDS

20 INSPIRING TRUE STORIES ABOUT PERSEVERANCE, BRAVERY, GENEROSITY & WINNING AGAINST ALL ODDS

HCK PRESS

PUBLISHED BY HCK PRESS

CONTENTS

Introduction v

1. Never Meet Your Heroes! 1
2. Wacky Superstitions 6
3. The Flower Pot 10
4. Lord Stanley's Font 16
5. Fighting Demons 22
6. The Return to Russia 27
7. Record-Breaking Hayley 33
8. Magical Marie 38
9. Does Height Matter? 42
10. A Late Starter 47
11. The Lockout of 2004 52
12. The Finnish Fighter 57
13. Realizing a Dream 62
14. The Great One 66
15. A little known story 71
16. Keeping the Faith 74
17. Playful Pranks 79
18. Sharpshooter 84
19. 'Boomer' Baun 89
20. Incredible Generosity 94

Conclusion 101
Also by HCK Press 103

Cover Image Design - Courtesy of a 99Designs.com Project

Bluberry Font Typeface - Licensed by Creativemarket.com

Print ISBN: 9781916815179

Ebook ISBN: 9781916815162

INTRODUCTION

In this book, you'll discover 20 incredible and intriguing short-stories from the wonderful world of Hockey. These stories span from Canada & the United States, and all around the world - as far as Europe and even Asia!

Each story is imbued with important lessons such as kindness, bravery, defeating adversity, faith in a higher power, or fun!

The stories aren't linked together or in order of time, so you can open the book at any chapter and start reading from anywhere you like, anytime you pick up the book!

We hope you enjoy these incredible, true short stories!

1

NEVER MEET YOUR HEROES!

The often used expression, 'never meet your hero,' reminds us that so often the people we put on pedestals do not (or cannot) always live up to our expectations, much to our disappointment, and one of Canadian hockey's greatest stars Brendan Shanahan knows exactly how this feels.

"Shanny" was born in Etobicoke, Ontario, in 1969. He grew up in Mimico, a neighbourhood in Toronto, Ontario, with his three brothers. As a boy, he was extremely competitive and excelled at most sports, especially lacrosse, before he realized his natural aptitude for hockey.

As a junior, Shanny played for the London Knights (of the Ontario Hockey League) and could hardly contain his excitement when skating at a rink in Toronto one summer, he discovered his idol, Rick Vaive, Maple Leafs captain and the first player in the team's history to score more than fifty goals in a season, was in the dressing room next door to his.

Despite being just fourteen years old, Shanny knew something of the demands on professional players before they hit the ice, the concentration and personal rituals necessary to keep them focussed, so he carefully chose what he thought would be the best time to go and ask the great man for his autograph, and maybe a few words of advice.

Unfortunately, Shanny would not get his autograph or anything else. For whatever reason, 'the Squid' was in no mood to meet his fans that day and unceremoniously told him to get out!

In the years that followed, Shanny developed into an extremely tough and dangerous player. He was drafted to the New Jersey Devils in the 1987 NHL Entry Draft and spent four seasons there. From the start, he was a force to be reckoned with.

Rick Vaive, meanwhile, had left the Maple Leafs in 1986 for the Buffalo Sabres, where he would end his career. When his team faced the 'Devils that season, he had no idea that he was up against an angry young man who had had four years to dwell on his dismissive, rude behaviour at the Toronto rink four years earlier.

Until Shanny and Squid faced off, the game had been a standard and reasonably even-tempered game, but at the moment Shanny squared up to Rick Vaive, everything changed. Shanny tore into him as if possessed, and it took two linesmen to drag him from the bemused older player; as he watched him being thrown into the penalty box, Squid asked the other 'Devils why on earth their teammate had attacked him with such fury.

It must have been a hard lesson to hear how his poor and dismissive attitude had had such an effect on that young fan at the start of his career, but he must have felt some relief that he clearly hadn't discouraged him!

And what a powerful, relentless player Shanny became! By the time he had given Rick Vaive something to think about, he had already played in the infamous 1987 World Junior Hockey Championships game between Canada and the Soviet Union that had descended into a twenty-minute brawl with the two sides being disqualified. The "Punch-Up in Piestany" (after the small Slovak town that hosted the tournament) was only brought to an abrupt end when officials turned off the arena lights.

Afterwards, he played for the St Louis Blues from 1991 to 1995, and then the Hartford Whalers; before winning three Stanley Cup championships and the King Clancy memorial trophy for his leadership and humanitarian work with the Detroit Red Wings.

His international career was just as impressive. After his disqualification from the 1987 World Junior Ice Hockey Championships, he won gold medals at the

1991 Canada Cup and the 1994 World Championship. He was captain of the national team at the 2006 Championships for their fourth-place finish.

He scored two goals in six games at the 1998 Winter Olympics held at Nagano, Japan, another fourth place, but at the Salt Lake Games in 2002, he won one of Canada's first Olympic gold medals.

In 2006, Shanny joined the New York Rangers (he was awarded the first Mark Messier Leadership Award that same year) and then finished his playing career with a return to the New Jersey Devils. At that time, he was the only player in the NHL to have scored 600 goals and 2000 penalty minutes.

In December 2009, just a month after his retirement, he was named the NHL's President of Hockey and Business Development, a role in which he was able to demonstrate the same tenacity and determination that he was known for as a player. He was initiated into the Hockey Hall of Fame in 2011. Then, in 2014, he was named president and alternate Governor of the Maple Leafs.

Throughout his long association with the sport, he has never forgotten how it felt to be treated so badly by someone he looked up to, and he has ensured that his own fans have never been subjected to that sort of treatment. On one occasion, a young man who asked for his autograph was none other than a young Justin Vaive, accompanied by his father, Rick. Although it did cross Shanny's mind to refuse, or worse, of course, Shanny obliged - not least, as he remarked in an interview sometime later, because he didn't want karma to come back to him.

2

WACKY SUPERSTITIONS

Sportsmen and women the world over are renowned for those personal superstitions and personal rituals that become an important part of their performances. Supporters and fans are fascinated by the toughest and most resilient sports stars' need to eat a particular dish before they can play, or their beliefs that they are doomed to fail if they forget to wear some particular underwear.

Former LSU (Louisiana State University) Tigers coach Les Miles would frequently rip up a handful of grass from the field on which his team would play in order to feel at one with the game, and Cuban baseball right fielder Yasiel Puig feels the need to lick his bat in an attempt to absorb its energy, while former Argentinian goalkeeper Sergio Goycochea's 'lucky charm' was to have a little pee immediately before every penalty kick he was expected to save.

Hockey is no different; Bruce Gardiner (who scored the very first goal for the Columbus Blue Jackets) would dunk the blade of his hockey stick into the locker room toilet before he played. Defenseman Chris Chelios, one of the longest-tenured players of the NHL, had to be the very man in the team to put on his jersey before each game, and Jocelyn Thibault, who played for the Quebec Nordiques, Colorado Avalanche and Pittsburgh Penguins (to name but a few) had to pour water over his head exactly six and a half minutes before the starting whistle.

Glenn Hall, one of the most renowned goaltenders in NHL history, had his own unique and unusual way of ensuring he played his best; he would vomit before each game.

This ritual began when he was playing in the Junior League as a youngster. He would become incredibly nervous and stressed in the build-up before each game, so much so that he could not help naturally throwing up. Afterwards, he would begin to feel better and calmer and eventually, before lacing up, he would wander into the bathroom to vomit and calm his nerves. In some interviews, he recalls standing on his head for sixty minutes afterwards.

Even in those early days, Glenn was a force to be reckoned with. He still holds the record for the most consecutive starts; between 6 October 1955 and 7 November 1963, he started and played for every minute of 502 games for two different sides - the

Detroit Red Wings, until 1956, when he was traded to the Chicago Black Hawks. This impressive run of games only came to an end when he pulled a muscle while getting dressed in the locker room.

Glenn won two Vezina Trophies (both shared) while he played for the Hawks and was the goaltender for their first victorious Stanley Cup run in twenty-three years, in 1961. Afterwards, he became known as "Mr Goalie" and developed his famous 'butterfly' technique, the preferred stance of goaltenders in the modern game. He found that leaving a gap between his pads helped him to get lower down in his efforts to save goals, even though, at a time when goaltenders did not wear masks, this was putting him at risk of serious injury. His teammates, seeing his white face waiting at the crease, tense with concentration, took to calling him 'Ghoulie,' a play on the Mr. Goalie name his fans had given him.

When asked about his strange pre-match ritual, he explained that, for the most part, it was quite natural, just the way in which his body coped with the increased adrenaline. On the occasions when he did not feel like he could vomit, he worried that maybe he wasn't taking that game seriously enough and, reminding himself that he was representing his family and loved ones, he would work himself into a state when he felt suitably nauseous - and then he would throw up.

Before getting ready to play, Glenn only ate because he had to, since he knew whatever he had swallowed would not stay down for very long, and he was never sick on the ice. There, he was able to control any waves of nausea with deep breathing, a trick he said he had learnt from basketball players.

One of his teammates, Glen Skov, said he always felt sorry for Mr. Goalie. He recalled how all of the team were nervous and that it was no bad thing because it kept them stimulated, their senses heightened, but he never came across anyone affected as badly as Glenn.

In 1975, Glenn was inducted into the Hockey Hall of Fame, and, in recent years, his contribution to the game has been reassessed. His steady reliability, courage, and forward-thinking play see him remembered in the top ten of every credible list of the NHL's best-ever goaltenders. It is, no doubt, for these achievements and his butterfly technique that he would rather be remembered, not for his bizarre pre-game ritual.

3

THE FLOWER POT

The Stanley Cup, known to many in the sport as the 'Holy Grail' or simply 'the Cup,' is the championship trophy presented each year to the captain of the victorious team after their series-winning game. This ceremony is conducted on the ice, and after the National Hockey League Commissioner has handed it to the captain, the tradition is for him to carry it around the rink, and then each player of the team makes his own lap of honour, holding the trophy aloft, to the jubilant cheers of the fans.

Unlike the trophies awarded in the other three major sports leagues in Canada and the United States (the Major League Baseball, the National Basketball Association and the National Football League), for whom a new cup is fashioned each season, the Stanley Cup is loaned by the Hockey Hall of Fame to the victorious club. Once it has been engraved with the names of the winning team, the managers and other important members of the club, it is handed over for the summer and then a few more selected days before it is returned to its home to be prepared (and, on occasion repaired) for the next season.

The Cup is the oldest trophy awarded annually to a professional sports franchise in North America, and it was Lord Frederick Stanley of Preston (and later 16th Earl of Derby), the third Governor General of Canada in 1892, who donated the original silverware.

After being appointed Governor in 1888, Lord Stanley visited western Canada, and he and his family quickly grew to love the country. He travelled extensively, immersed himself in the customs and culture of the country, and became a passionate ice hockey enthusiast. His sons, Arthur and Algernon, took to hockey and played in amateur leagues in Ottawa; Arthur even helped to form a new team, the Ottawa Rideau Hall Rebels and brought the sport (with others) to Great Britain.

It was the Stanley family's idea to donate a trophy, and after attending Ottawa Hockey Club's victory celebrations in 1892, he commissioned a traditional rose bowl made of silver. It measures 18,5 cm (7,28 inches) in height and 29 cm (11,42 inches) in width. It was crafted in Sheffield, South Yorkshire, but Lord Stanley purchased it from a silversmith in the Piccadilly area of London, G. R. Collins and Company for ten guineas.

He had the words "Dominion Hockey Challenge Cup" engraved on the outside rim of one side of the Cup and "From Stanley of Preston" on the other. He intended for it to be awarded to the top amateur hockey team in Canada and made five rules fit its award; it was to be returned to the trustees in good order, and each winning team could have its name and date engraved on a silver ring to be fitted to the trophy - at its own expense, it was to remain a challenge cup and could not become the property of a team - however many times they might win it, it's trustees have absolute authority in that case of any dispute over the winning of the Cup, and if when a trustee chooses to leave or is unable to continue his duties, the remaining trustee should nominate a replacement.

The first trustees were Sheriff John Sweetland and Philip D Ross, appointed by Lord Stanley, and they presented the Cup for the first time in 1893 to the Montreal Amateur Athletic Association on behalf of Montreal Hockey Club as they were top of the league at the end of the season and so, the trustees believed, the best team in Canada. The champions of the Ontario Hockey Association, another league that had been established, were understandably affronted since they hadn't been given any opportunity to play Montreal. The newspapers took up their cause (and, for the first time, a piece in the Ottawa Journal referred to it as 'the Stanley Cup'). As a result, the rules and regulations were revisited, and it became a fairer competition.

Unfortunately, Lord Stanley never had the joy of watching a championship game or presenting his trophy personally. His brother, the Earl of Derby, died in 1993, and he had to return to Britain as heir to the title and estate.

In 1895, the Montreal Victorias won the league title and were awarded the Stanley Cup, but were challenged by Montreal HC and, after decisively beating them in a 5 - 1 thriller, the challengers were crowned champions.

The following year, another cup tradition began. The Winnipeg Victorias, champions of the Manitoba Hockey League, introduced the custom for the winning side to drink champagne from the bowl.

In 1907, the Stanley Cup had two champions. The season had ended with it being awarded to the Montreal Wanderers, who saw off a challenge from the New Glasgow Cubs in December 1906. The Kenora Thistles challenged the Wanderers in January, and with several borrowed 'ringers,' future Hockey Hall of Fame stars Art Ross, Tom Hooper, and Tommy Phillips beat the Wanderers for the Cup.

When the Wanders won the ECAHA (Eastern Canada Amateur Hockey Association) leave title, undefeated in ten games, they challenged the Kenora Thistles for the Cup. It was not an easy game to arrange; both teams accused the other of wanting to use ringers, but two games were arranged at the Winnipeg Arena, and, despite the Kenora Thistles winning one of them, the Wanders ultimately triumphed.

The winning team's names were engraved inside the trophy (only two teams share the honour of having their names in the bowl of the original Cup), and, to mark the occasion, the team and club members had a selection of photographs taken at the Montreal studio of Jimmy Rice, a photographer who took many iconic pictures of hockey players with his box camera in the first half of the 20th century.

Afterwards, somehow, the Stanley Cup was stolen but, when no ransom was forthcoming, the miserable thieves just left it on Jimmy Rice's doorstep and, when neither team nor trustees came to collect it, the photographer's practical wife used it as a planter for her red geraniums until the new season started later that year.

Another, more likely, version of the story is that the team simply forgot the Cup and left it at the studio, and, after it had remained there, uncollected, for several weeks, Mrs. Rice decided to put her plants in it as a display for the photography studio's shop window. Either way, it came to no harm, and it was back with the trustees, ready for its next presentation.

In 1924, the Montreal Wanderers won the Cup again, and they clearly hadn't learned anything from the events of 1907. When the vehicle they were travelling in had to stop for a flat tyre to be mended, the team waited at the roadside with their trophy. Once they were back on board and homeward bound, to their horror, they realized they had left the 'holy grail' behind. Fortunately, when they went back, it was exactly where they had left it.

4

LORD STANLEY'S FONT

The current Stanley Cup is not topped with the rose bowl that Lord Stanley purchased from the Piccadilly silver dealer in 1892. The price-less original is held in Lord Stanley's Vault in the Eason Great Hall at the Hockey Hall of Fame in Toronto.

The early winners began adding tiered rings engraved with the names of the team, its coaches and other important personnel, and then several narrow bands - also engraved - were added. It became so tall and narrow that it was sometimes referred to as the "stovepipe cup."

In 1919, the NHL suspended all games due to the Spanish Flu outbreak, an epidemic that claimed the lives of 50,000 Canadians and 657,000 Americans, with more casualties than World War I, World War II, the Korean War and the Vietnam War combined, most of whom were young adults aged between 29 and 40. The

Cup records that terrible time with the words, "Season not played."

In 1958, a barrel was designed so that five silver bands could be engraved with the details of thirteen winners. Every thirteen years, the top band is removed to be displayed at the Lord Stanley Vault with the original trophy, a new blank band is added to the bottom, and the other bands move up the barrel. In this way, each champion's engraved details should remain on the Cup for sixty-five years.

1962 was a bad year for the Cup itself; it was won by the Toronto Maple Leafs, but a Canadien fan almost managed to steal it, saying he was taking it back to Montreal "where it belongs." During the Maple Leafs jubilant celebrations, the trophy fell into a bonfire, and the embarrassed club had to pay for it to be repaired.

The following year, NHL President Clarence Campbell had the trophy assessed by conservation experts, and it was decided that it was too brittle to continue withstanding the exuberant celebrations at the end of each season. A 'Presentation Cup' replica was lovingly created from a silver and nickel alloy, stands at 89,54 cm (35,25 inches) high, and weighs a hefty 15,5 kg (34,5 lbs). It came into use in 1970, and the original was retired at the same time.

The NHL commissioned a third 'Replica Cup' from Montreal silversmith Louise St Jacques in 1993, and this is on display at the Hockey Hall of Fame while the current Presentation Cup is in service elsewhere.

Montreal Canadiens center Henri Richard had his name engraved on the Cup eleven times, the most as a player, but Jean Beliveau is included ten times as a player of the same team- and another seven times as an executive. Several names have been misspelt over the years (including the word 'Boston' when the Boston Bruins won the 1971- 72 championship and the word 'Islanders' after a New York Islanders' win), and another Canadiens player, goaltender Jacques Plante, won the trophy five consecutive years and his name is engraved differently each time.

The youngest player to be named is Larry Hillman, who was eighteen, two months and nine days when the Detroit Red Wings lifted the trophy in 1955, and the oldest is Chris Chelios, forty- six and six months when he won with the same team, more than half a century later (in 2008).

There are fifteen women's names on the Cup. The first is Marguerite Norris, the first female team executive in the NHL and President of Detroit Red Wings at the time of their 1955 win, and the second, the only Canadian, is the philanthropist Sonia Scurfield, one of the co-owners of the victorious Calgary Flames in 1989.

Red Kelly won eight Stanley Cups in his long career, and after he lifted the trophy with the Maple Leafs in 1964, he posed for photographs with his new little son sitting in the bowl. Afterwards, he realized the baby had had a small accident while sitting there and afterwards; it always amused him to see the winning team reverently sipping champagne from what had been an ad hoc potty for his family!

Since 1995, it has become traditional for each player on the winning team to have their own 'private' day with the trophy, although at least one Hockey Hall of Fame representative is always in attendance nearby, and, as a result, the Cup has found itself filled with dog food by Clark Gillies of the New York Islanders who insisted his 'good' dog deserved the honour of dining in such style in 1980 (Buddy, the black Labrador retriever belonging to Sean O'Donnell of the Anaheim Ducks had the same in 2007), tested for buoyancy in the swimming pools of the Pittsburgh's Penguins Mario Lemieux (in 1991) and Montreal Canadiens star, Patrick Roy (in 1993), and filled with chocolate milk for Los Angeles Kings winger Dustin Brown's two boys to enjoy.

It has been filled with raw clams and oysters whilst wearing a baseball cap and false moustache by New York Rangers Brian Noonan and Nick Kypreos in 1994, popcorn - during a trip to the cinema for New Jersey Devil's goalie Martin Brodeur and his family in 2003, *pitepalt* - Swedish stuffed potato dumplings - when Red Wings champion Tomas Holmstrom brought it back to his native Sweden in 2008 and, on that occasion, it was also used in the baptism of his niece.

One player, defenseman Jack Johnson, originally from Indiana, had always promised his children that if he was ever in the team that won the playoff championship, they would eat ice cream out of the Stanley Cup on his special day.

After sixteen seasons with five different teams, Jack agreed to sign a single-year contract with the Colorado Avalanche in October 2021 and helped the team win their first NHL championship in twenty-one years with a six game victory against the Tampa Bay Lightning in the final. That day, he became the nineteenth player in the league's history to win the Cup after playing a thousand games (it was his thousand and twenty-fourth).

Jack had no intention of forgetting his promise, and after checking with the Hockey Hall of Fame, the Johnson family enjoyed an extra large and very delicious ice cream sundae served from the Holy Grail at an Ohio ice cream parlour. But there was another very special purpose they had in mind for the Stanley Cup while it was in their care.

Jack and Kelly, his wife, had already arranged baptisms for their three children that very same weekend and with the Cup in their possession, it seemed fated to have it blessed as an honorary font for that significant occasion. This was not the first time it had been used in baptism ceremonies for the sons and daughters of the players; another Colorado Avalanche defenseman, Sylvain Lefebvre's little daughter, was the first in 1996. Then Brecken Archibald, the three-week-old son of Pittsburg Penguins right-winger Josh Archibald, received the sacred sacrament, with a difference, in August 2017.

The Johnson children were baptized in a private ceremony attended by Super Bowl champion and Packers linebacker A J Hawk, Jack's brother-in-law and other family guests, and afterwards, Kelly released a photograph that captured the minister tending to the children with holy water drawn from the bowl at the top of the trophy.

The Cup has also been a part of wedding ceremonies for players and their families and, as a symbol of the sport that has brought such success for the dedication and sacrifices of the players and the loved ones who have supported them, it is a wonderful opportunity to give thanks for the sport that has given so much joy, comradeship and material rewards.

5

FIGHTING DEMONS

Chris Nilan was born in West Roxbury, Massachusetts, in 1958 and, with his tough upbringing, growing up on the streets of Boston, he had already become known as "Knuckles" or "Nuck." By the time he started his professional career as a right-wing for the Montreal Canadiens, he was already a formidable enforcer.

He soon became known for his extremely aggressive play and would not be intimidated by anyone. From the start, he grappled with some of the most feared bruisers of the time; Terry "Tasmanian Devil" O'Reilly, Stan "Bulldog" Jonathan, "Big Mac" Jim McKenzie and Stu "the Grim Reaper" Grimson. When he looked back over his career, he said he never made the mistake of underestimating any of them and went into attack, knowing full well that they were looking to do exactly the same to him.

In 1986, in a particularly badly-natured game between the Canadiens and their bitterest rivals, the Boston Bruins, Chris had been sent off for fighting and, as he was leaving the rink, Ken Linseman, on the Bruins bench, shouted something at him. Chris went for him, and this started an all-out brawl that wasn't just confined to the ice; players from both sides fought against each other, grappling in the corridor that led to the locker rooms. There was no doubt that Chris had started the uproar, and for this, he received a three-game suspension (two other players were also disciplined afterwards). The fight had been so fierce that executives responsible for the Bruins' arena, the Boston Garden, felt compelled to install plexiglass that separated the Bruins bench from the route to the locker room.

During a long career, from 1979 to 1992, Chris won the Stanley Cup with Montreal and, fulfilling his childhood dream, played for the Boston Bruins. With them, he set the NHL record for the most penalty minutes in a game against the Hartford Whalers. He had seasons with the New York Rangers, back with the Boston Bruins and ended his career with the Montreal Canadiens. He had scored 110 goals - "Not bad for an enforcer," as he once remarked - 115 assists and a whopping 3,043 penalty minutes.

Despite finding fame and fortune with his prowess as a hard man on the ice, the years of scoring goals, putting up a formidable defence and not least, his recorded 316 fights took their toll. He had picked up several injuries over the years, including a broken ankle that forced him to miss his controversial selection for the 1991 NHL All-Star Game. Enduring more than thirty surgeries left him with an addiction to painkillers.

After retiring from the game, Chris struggled to find his way. He had unresolved mental health issues as well as his addiction to prescription drugs, and when he was no longer able to get that medication, he turned to alcohol and heroin and found himself in a downward spiral, desperate and ashamed, struggling to see any way out.

He says he hit rock bottom when he was injecting himself with heroin in a hotel toilet after feeling particularly sick one day. When he came around, he could see that he had left the needle in his arm. Alarmed, he tried to stand up, but his legs gave way beneath him; he fell over and knocked himself out.

As he came around a second time, he realized he could not continue to live in this way and, just as his mother had taught him when he was a little boy, he knelt and prayed for help.

It was a long road to recovery; Chris has called it the toughest fight of his life. He has endured two spells in rehab, he has come to terms with his addiction, managed his anger and taken steps to atone for the hurt he caused his family.

Chris's life has since taken a very different direction since those dark days. He became involved in a major campaign to help stop bullying in schools after hearing about the tragic suicide of a young girl in Massachusetts. He has visited schools to talk to students and promoted the clear message that they should not just stand by if they see bullying behaviour but tell the perpetrator to stop or tell a teacher or responsible adult about their concerns. He was able to speak from his own childhood experiences and stressed that though he had been a very aggressive player and legendary enforcer, he was proud that he had never been a bully.

He was delighted to do his bit for the military and made several visits to troops serving in Afghanistan with other former NHL players to help raise morale. He has also made a point of helping several charities and good causes, sharing his own experiences and supporting fundraising appeals and, through his recovery, he began to realize that he was a really good communicator.

In 2013, he began hosting his own radio show, but more recently, he and former NHL center Tim Stapleton began hosting a podcast in which they discuss sporting issues, particularly those relating to hockey, in their own inimitable and entertaining way.

Chris is also deeply committed to helping another cause. In recent years, the effects of sporting blows on the head and brain have been studied by medical researchers and this kind of traumatic brain injury is believed to be a possible contributor to the progressive and fatal brain disease CTE (Chronic Traumatic Encephalopathy) and if this is the case, many sports stars may be suffering from this condition. Currently, it cannot be diagnosed until after the patient has died. When Chris learned that his old friend, fellow enforcer Bob Probert, had been found to be suffering from CTE after his death in 2010, he agreed to help the research programme, knowing there was a strong possibility that he might have the disease.

Chris is regularly tested and assessed and has promised his brain to CTE research after his death. It is hoped that with better understanding, players of contact sports like hockey can be better protected, diagnosed and, perhaps, cured if they develop symptoms. If it is found that he does not have CTE, understanding why not will be just as valuable, doctors have said.

Living a quiet life in Montreal, committed to good causes with his addiction issues behind him, the fans who watched him in his heyday must find it hard to see him as that angry young man, an enforcer and legendary hard man of the ice.

6

THE RETURN TO RUSSIA

Pavel Datsyuk was born on 20 July 1978 in Sverdlovsk (now Yekaterinburg, since 1991), an industrial city in west-central Russia and 1,667 km (1,036 miles) from Moscow. His father was a delivery truck driver, and his mother worked long hours managing the canteen of a munitions factory. Pavel was a quiet, well-behaved boy, and he and his sister, Larisa, enjoyed an ordinary Russian childhood.

As well as having a passion for toy cars, Pavel loved to play sports. He was competitive, he showed a natural aptitude for soccer and, from the start, he was a true team player.

Pavel's father was an enthusiastic hockey fan who would watch any game he could find on the television. He took his little son to the ice rink in the courtyard at their apartment complex, where a volunteer coach named Vladimir Sitnikov had started training local youngsters and had formed a junior team.

At just five years old, Pavel was hooked. But playing with *Dadya* ("uncle") Vova, as they called their coach, was hard work in more ways than one. The youngsters all helped to scrape the heavy snow from the surface of the ice and then prepared it with a sprinkling of water before they could start to play, but once they were ready, they dashed around the rink, learning skills and speed, and playing games until their fingers and toes were numb with cold. Pavel's father watched and cheered!

And it was cold! The bitter Russian winters in Yekaterinburg could drop to temperatures of -40° C (-40 F), but this didn't stop the resilient little Soviets from skating every night until it was dark.

Pavel did not have ice hockey skates and used his sister's old figure skates to begin with. Despite being teased by some of his teammates, he thinks they helped him to develop agility and swiftness that some of the others lacked, and, always concerned about breaking his stick, he became a creative, intelligent player, able to quickly work out any opportunities to fox his opponents rather than fighting to score.

As soon as he was old enough, Pavel was enrolled in the nearest children's sports program. It was a fair distance from the Datsyuk home, and he was forced to travel by train across the city, with two transfers, carrying his heavy bag of kit. He would sit on his preferred Number 13 train, dreaming of a future when he was a great player and developed a determination to succeed.

Pavel loved his time at the *Yunost* ("youth") hockey school, but again, it was hard. He was expected to demonstrate his commitment by working out and practicing every day, and each summer, he spent two months away from his family at the Orlenok hockey camp for intensive training.

In 1994, Pavel's mother passed away. It was an incredibly difficult time for the family, but he found some solace in the game he loved and knew his mother would be proud of the progress he was making. He had started to participate in tournaments, and he was beginning to realize his worth as a player.

Pavel became professional in 1996 when he was eighteen, and, to illustrate the different life experiences of young players in the East and the West, he spent his entire first paycheck on a colour television. He started his career with his local team, Yekaterinburg's CKA, then moved to Dynamo-Energiya in the Russian Premier League and helped them win the Championship in his first season.

He quickly found his stride with Dynamo and became such a threat that other teams in the league had to ensure they had a player dedicated to shadowing him, ready to shut down his innovative play. In 1998, however, a hard blow to the knee resulted in a severe injury. Despite immediate surgery, it seemed that Pavel's career might well be over, but after a period of gruelling physiotherapy and rehabilitation, he was back on the ice and, in 2000, with AK Bars Kazan in the Russian Elite League.

Pavel's expertise had come to the attention of the Detroit Red Wings director of European Scouting, Håkan Andersson, in the summer of 1998 when he had visited Moscow to scout another player. Pavel wasn't the obvious choice; he was small for a hockey player at 180 cm (5 ft 11 in), shy, and he had an unusual gait - "like a pelican," one of his Russian coaches remarked, with good humour.

When he heard that he had made the 6th round draft at pick 171, Pavel thought it had to be a joke and wouldn't believe it until he saw it printed in the newspaper the following morning. But it was true, and Pavel left Mother Russia for the West.

When he arrived in Detroit, he was very fortunate to have other Russian players on the team, Igor Laionov and Sergei Fedorov, who befriended him on and off the ice and gave him invaluable support and guidance to help him adapt to a strange new country and a very different lifestyle.

On the ice, he quickly demonstrated his playmaking skills with eleven goals in his rookie season and three goals and assists in the Red Wings' third Stanley Cup championship in six years. Pavel took his turn and carried the trophy around the ice, wearing his number 13 shirt; the number he had chosen as it was the number of one of the trains he had taken across Yekaterinburg to his hockey school, a reminder of his roots.

When Igor Fedorov left the Red Wings in 2003, Pavel took his center place and, with Boyd Devereaux (who had joined the Red Wings in the same season as Pavel) and Matthieu Dandenault on either side, the famous Red Wing' D Line' came to be. The following year, during the 2004- 2005 NHL Lockout, Pavel returned to Russia to play for Moscow Dynamo in the KHL (Kontinental Hockey League) and, with them, won the Championship.

Back with the Red Wings the following season, his creative, exciting play made him one of the most popular stars in the league. Those who played alongside him respected his intelligence, his quiet determination and his modesty; he was always uncomfortable at the prospect of long interviews for the media or promotional activities and preferred to spend his time away from the ice with his family or playing soccer or tennis.

Although he appreciated his time in Detroit and had developed a deep fondness for the city, he was always first and foremost Russian. In 2006, he founded a youth hockey school near his hometown where talented young players from all over Russia could be coached and taught by some of the leading international coaches and players.

In March 2015, Pavel was in the first year of a three-year $22,5 million contract when he felt his ankle buckle as he blocked a puck. He missed several games while he had physiotherapy, but still in some pain, he returned to the ice for the playoffs.

While he was in Yekaterinburg for the offseason, he realized the injury was more serious than he had first thought and flew back to the States for exploratory surgery. During this procedure, it became clear that he had ruptured two tendons and after reparative surgery and therapy, he recovered and returned to the team.

After he had scored his 300th goal in the 2015-16 season, he began to think that it was time for him to go home to Russia. "I'm not thinking about my ankle, I'm thinking about my heart," he said when he announced his decision on 18 June 2016.

Since he returned to his homeland, Pavel played for three seasons in the KHL with Saint Petersburg, and with them, he lifted the Gagarin Cup (aptly named after the first man in space, Yuri Gagarin). He finished his career with two years at Yekaterinburg, a promise he had made to himself many years before and since retiring in 2022, he has devoted himself to player development in Yekaterinburg, helping young athletes to achieve their dreams just like he did.

7

RECORD-BREAKING HAYLEY

"People would say, 'Girls don't play hockey, girls don't skate.' I would say, 'Watch this.'"

- Hayley Wickenheiser

Considered by many the greatest female hockey player of all time, Hayley Wickenheiser was born in Shaunavon, a town in southwest Saskatchewan, in 1978. Both her parents were physical education teachers, and when they took their little girl to an indoor rink, she took to the game straight away.

The family moved to Calgary, Alberta, and Hayley continued to play, but, as before, she had to play in boys' teams since there were no girls' teams available for her. It took some dedication and determination; there were no female changing rooms, so she had to get ready in the bathrooms, and it was hard for her to feel like an accepted member of the team. She always had her hair cut short, hoping to fit in and, of course, once she was on the ice, she felt great and that she belonged.

Hayley showed great promise from the start, and with the tenacity she had developed, she quickly became a dynamic and dangerous player. From her position as center, she was a superb forward player with a fierce slap shot, and she brought a physical element to the game that was unusual for women players at the time. Although she would agree that she wasn't the fastest skater, her powerful stride and superb balance made it almost impossible for her opponents to take the puck from her.

In 1991, Hayley represented Alberta in the ice hockey 18-and-under category at the Canada Winter Games and, despite being the youngest and the smallest player (she was 1,5 metres, or 5 feet tall), she scored the game-winning goal in the final and, alongside her gold medal, she was named 'Most Valuable Player' in that game.

In 1994, at age fifteen, Hayley was called to Canada's national women's team. Her first international tournament was the World Championship at Lake Placid, New York. She played in three games and was thrilled to be one of the gold medal-winning champions.

Hayley took a more prominent role in Canada's gold medal victory at the International Ice Hockey Federation (IIHF) 1997 Women's World Hockey Championship in Kitchener, Ontario. She scored nine points and an assist in the overtime final against the United

States team, and this earned her a place on the tournament's all-star team.

As captain, Hayley led her team to glory in the 1999 (held at Espoo, Finland) and the 2000 (Mississauga, Canada) World Championship but was ruled out of the 2001 tournament with a knee injury. At that time, Canada dominated the international women's game until 2005, when they were beaten to silver medal place by the US team.

Back to her best, in 2007 at Winnipeg, Hayley (as captain) scored eight goals and six assists, a record for the Canadian team at a women's world championship, and was named Most Valuable Player. She led her team to victory again at Vermont in the United States in 2012.

Hayley did not just excel in the World Championships; she is a four-time Olympic gold medalist. In her first outing at the Nagano Winter Olympic Games in 1998, she had to be satisfied with silver when the Canadian team was defeated by the Americans in the final.

Four years later, at the Salt Lake City Olympics, Hayley was on the gold medal-winning team and the Americans were left with silver. She was voted Most Valuable Player and, with ten points, she was the leading scorer and star of the show.

Hayley became the first woman to play full-time in a professional men's team (other than a goaltender) in 2003 when she joined the third-division Finnish club

Salamat. She was keen to challenge herself to see how far she could go in the sport, and she battled on the ice against much taller and heavier players and even managed to score.

In the 2006 Turin Olympics, Canada's biggest rivals were - as usual - the powerful and accomplished women of the US team, favourites for gold that year, but in an exciting turnaround, Sweden beat the Americans in the semi-final and then, in the final, Hayley's team won gold again. Recollecting that time, she said, "That was a very important time for us as a team. It was our second gold medal in a row, following Salt Lake City, and really established ourselves as the best team in the world." On a personal level, despite picking up injuries to her elbow and foot, Hayley managed to beat her own personal performance from four years earlier with seventeen points - and another Most Valuable Player (MVP) award.

After another gold medal win at Vancouver in 2010, Hayley was selected as flag bearer for the opening ceremony at the 2014 Winter Olympics in Sochi, Russia. Her team stormed their way to gold again.

Hayley's Olympic sporting achievements are not just confined to hockey; in 2000, she represented Canada in the softball competition, and despite a decisive victory over Italy, the team did not make it into the second round.

In 2017, at the age of 38, Hayley made the decision to retire from hockey in a bid to spend more time with her son, Noah, and attend medical school at the University of Toronto; her long-held ambition had always been to become a doctor. In addition to studying, Hayley accepted an Assistant General Manager role at the Toronto Maple Leafs with a strong focus on player development.

When she was finally inducted into the Hockey Hall of Fame, she was the seventh female player to receive the honour. Hayley was incredibly proud to be listed alongside the players she idolized as a youngster, and when she reflected on those days, she realized how far and inclusive hockey had become. Of course, there is always room for improvement, but women's hockey has come a long way in her lifetime.

8

MAGICAL MARIE

Marie-Philip Paulin was born on 28 March, 1991 in Beauceville, Quebec. When she was very small, her parents took her to figure skating classes, but Marie had no time for that. More than anything, she wanted to play hockey like her big brother, Pierre-Alexandre.

She started hockey at the age of five, and from that day there was no stopping her. When she was eleven, she took the opportunity to see the Canadian Women's Team defeat the United States team at the 2002 Salt Lake City Olympic Games and win gold medals, and she began to dream that maybe one day, she, too, might represent her country.

Marie was fully aware that it would take hard work, perseverance and dedication to succeed, so she practiced her game and developed her skills until, at the age of twelve, she began playing competitively.

In 2007, Marie joined the Canada national team program, and the following January, she played in the inaugural World Under 18 Championship at Prince George, British Columbia. She scored four goals and an assist in two games against Sweden's national women's team and was named the tournament's top forward.

Marie won her first Olympic gold medal at the Vancouver Winter Games in 2010 and began her collegiate career at Boston University later that year. She studied psychology and became the captain of the women's hockey team. The team quickly improved under her leadership and made it to the National Championship in her freshman year.

After graduating from Boston University, Marie enrolled at Dawson College in Montreal to continue her education and joined Les Canadiennes de Montreal in the Women's Hockey League (CWHL). The team won the Clarkson Cup twice under her leadership, and she was named the CWHL Most Valuable Player three times.

At the end of the 2015- 16 season, Marie was the inaugural winner of the Jayna Hefford Trophy, which was awarded annually to the CWHL's most outstanding player, as voted for by the players. She received the same trophy for her 2017 -18 and 2018- 19 seasons.

In 2019, Canadian hockey was rocked by allegations of sexual assault by some players on the Junior national team and the funds from which compensation payments were paid to the victims that had made the allegations. The management of Hockey Canada was questioned by a parliamentary committee, several of the top executives were forced to resign, the government cut funding, and sponsors quickly distanced themselves.

Marie, captain of the national women's team, quickly spoke out. She recognized that she and her teammates were role models for young women and girls and vowed to ensure women's rights would be protected in the sport for players, fans, and anyone else associated with women's hockey. She felt compelled to speak out again in that same December when the IIHF pulled the women's under 18 championship - while the men's world junior championship received the funding and support to go ahead.

The lack of funding, as well as difficulties with the governing bodies, resulted in the Canadian Women's Hockey League being discontinued. This was a real step backward for the sport. Without regular competition, the advances made over the decades seemed to have made little progress and Marie, as captain of Les Canadiennes de Montreal, was among the players who would campaign and work for a new league for women's teams.

She always pressed critics to go and watch the female athletes playing hockey, knowing they would be pleasantly surprised at the quality of play and that even the most chauvinistic of fans can become hooked when they have experienced the excitement of a live game.

At the 2021 IIHF Women's World Championship, Marie scored the golden goal in the overtime period that gave Canada a 3-2 win over the United States and her team's first gold medal at the championships since 2012.

At the 2022 Beijing Olympics, Canada beat the United States, and with her third gold medal, Marie was affectionately dubbed "Captain Clutch." She is the sole hockey player in the entire world - male or female - to have scored goals in four consecutive Olympic finals (with seven goals)!

That summer, she became the player development consultant for the Montreal Canadiens, a new challenge in which she helped players develop their skills.

April 2023, Marie scored her 100th goal for Canada (then scored another) in the IIHF Women's World Championship against Czechia.

Although she values her privacy, in May 2023, Marie announced her engagement to her teammate, Laura Stacey. Months later, they both signed with the new PWHL team based in Montreal, a great partnership on and off the ice.

9

DOES HEIGHT MATTER?

The average height of an NHL player is 1,85 metres (just over 6 foot 1 inches). Taller players have a greater reach and tend to have more power and the ability to hit harder, but shorter players are more agile and often faster on the ice.

Traditionally, smaller players make better wingers. In these forward positions, natural acceleration and pace are vital, and if the player is able to anticipate the game, they soon become an integral part of the team. Despite this, many franchises are reluctant to chance on those who don't measure up on the height chart.

One player who really fought for his career was Martin St Louis.

Martin was born in Laval, Quebec in 1975. As a youngster, he was a natural on the ice and played in the 1988 Quebec International Pee-Wee Hockey tournament with his local team.

He started his college career at the University of Vermont and studied business management. There, with the Vermont Catamounts, his game really came into its own; he was the standout player and broke the record for points scored for the team with 267 points, then became an NCAA All-Star. During his time at Vermont, he was nominated for the Hobey Baker Award three times.

With such an outstanding college career behind him, he had every right to expect a raft of interest from the best NHL teams to choose from, but it was not to be; Martin's height, at 173 cm (5ft 8 in), was against him.

Undrafted, Martin joined the Cleveland Lumberjacks on the understanding that he would be free to leave if an NHL team offered him a contract. After scoring 50 points in 56 games, he signed for the Calgary Flames, and he played in their AHL (American Hockey League) affiliate, the Saint John Flames and reached the Calder Cup finals with them.

When Martin left Calgary in 2000, a number of clubs were interested in signing him, but he chose the Tampa Bay Lightning in the belief that there, he would have better opportunities to play full games in the NHL.

It was not an easy transition, and, at first, Martin struggled to shine and was not always listed in the lineup to begin with. He had tried to improve his game and had made several changes to his style of play, but he began to realize that he needed to trust his own instincts, and with a more instinctive approach, he began scoring again.

After recovering from a broken leg in the 2001-02 season, he found his stride and became a lynchpin of a team that was going places! In 2003, they won their first playoff series, and at the end of the following season, Martin gained the most points in the league and was awarded the Art Ross Trophy.

In 2004, Martin led the Lightning to an even greater glory - the Stanley Cup. Already popular with the fans, the diminutive right winger was named a first-team All-Star. As the NHL's most valuable player, he was awarded the Hart Memorial Trophy and the Lester B Pearson Award in the players' vote.

Martin spent the cancelled NHL season playing for HC Lausanne in Switzerland's National League A and scored an impressive 25 points in 23 games. Back in the States for the 2006- 07 season, he took more than 100 points and played his 500th game. He was the first Lightning player to appear in three All-Star Games, and when the team captain was injured, Martin was named alternate captain going into the next season.

His success continued; in the 2007-08 season, he attained his 500th career point and his fifth All-Star appearance, then scored another 94 points in the next season. At the end of the 2009-2010 season, he finished with only 12 penalty minutes and, as the most gentle-manly player, he received the Lady Byng Memorial Trophy (this was the third time he had been nominated for the award). He received the same award in 2011. That same year, despite having to endure facial surgery after being hit by a teammate during a practice game and missing five games, he made his sixth All-Star appearance and was within a whisker of winning a second Hart Memorial Trophy.

It was no surprise that Martin had become a fan favourite. He was named captain of the Lightning at the start of the 2013- 14 season and, that November, played his 1,000 NHL game. The team's general manager, Steve Yzerman, was also general manager for Canada's national team, and he decided not to include Martin for his 2014 Winter Olympic Games team.

Martin was devastated not to have the opportunity to play for his country, and when his Lightning teammate, Steven Stamkos, was unable to play through injury, he was able to take his place. At Sochi, he played in five of Canada's six games, including their victorious final against Sweden.

Although he was delighted to be an Olympic gold medalist, Martin couldn't help feeling let down by his manager. He felt he had done all he could to warrant being a first-choice pick for his national team and felt that if Steven Stamkos did not have full confidence in his abilities, he didn't want to stay; he wanted to leave.

Locked into a contract, his only option was to be traded with a player from another team and in March 2014, he was exchanged for Ryan Callahan and, to the

Lightning fans' disgust, he left to join the New York Rangers.

Although he was a driving force in the team's success in their run to the Stanley Cup final, Martin's mother died unexpectedly. With the emotional strain and competing against players almost half his age, he was coming to the end of his career. 2014- 15 was to be his last NHL season.

The bad feeling about his departure melted away when Martin made his return with his new team. Before the game, a tribute was displayed on the large screens, and when he skated onto the ice, his old fans gave him a standing ovation. In interviews years later, he would speak of his regret about leaving Tampa and the way it happened.

Martin announced his retirement in July 2015, and since then, he has started a coaching career. He was eventually inducted into the Hockey Hall of Fame in 2018, and the Tampa Bay Lightning Hall of Fame as a member of its first class in 2023. Perhaps the most touching tribute to the man and the player was the decision made in January 2017 that Martin's number 26 was the first to be retired in Lightning history.

10

A LATE STARTER

Joe Mullen was born in New York City in 1957. He grew up in the 'Hell's Kitchen' neighbourhood on the West Side of Midtown Manhattan. It was a very rough area where drugs and gangs were a serious problem.

Joe's father worked on ice and maintenance at Madison Square Garden and, as small children, Joe and his brothers, Ken, Tom Jr, and Brian, often hung out at the arena, trying to fire shots against each other with old sticks.

At the age of five, Joe started playing roller hockey on a concrete schoolyard court using a roll of electrical tape in place of a puck! He developed a fine sense of balance and a fearless attitude that he was able to transfer to the ice when, at age ten, he swapped his four-wheeled roller skates for ice skates.

There was no stopping Joe. He joined the Metropolitan Junior Hockey Association at fourteen, one of the league's youngest players, and in his four seasons, he was one of the top goal scorers.

Although he had spent most of his young life whizzing about on skates and developing skills that had been able to quickly and effectively transfer to the ice, his late start to the game would become another obstacle for him to overcome.

The vast majority of NHL players start skating at a very early age, some before they are out of diapers. This means they are proficient and instinctive skaters by the time they start to play hockey, ideally at around five years old (most hockey clubs will not accept members under five).

It is unfortunate that children who are not exposed to the sport as young children are rarely able to break into hockey, but there are always exceptions like Joe. Bep Guidolin was a late learner, but due to so many players being called for military service in the Second World War, he was able to start a hockey career before being called up himself. Rod Langway started at thirteen, and Yvon Pierre Lambert received his first pair of skates when he was thirteen but didn't play organized hockey until he was fifteen.

In 1975, Joe accepted a partial scholarship to Boston College to play for the Eagles hockey program, but after he had scored 34 points in 24 games in his first year, he was given a full scholarship.

He excelled at Boston and led the Eagles to the Eastern College Athletic Conference Championship (ECCA) in 1978. He was named an All-Star of the NCAA Tournament that same year. Although the Eagles lost to their old rivals, Boston University, Joe was pleased to have scored a goal against them.

During his collegiate career, he set school records of 110 goals and 212 points and was the team captain in the 1978- 79 season. He was named All-ECAC, the All-New England and NCAA All-American teams and awarded the Walter Brown Award as the best American-born player in New England.

Boston College has not forgotten its dynamic and speedy New Yorker. He was inducted into the school's Varsity Club Hall of Fame in 1998, and the following season, his number 21 jersey was retired.

Despite his obvious talent and impressive achievements, Joe wasn't drafted after finishing at Boston; the preference tended to be for young men from more traditional hockey-playing states, who had been skating and then playing since they were about the size of a hockey stick and, at 175 cm (5 feet 9 inches), his height was against him. He was offered the opportunity to play for the legendary "Miracle on Ice" 1980 United States Olympic Team, but he had other responsibilities. He needed to help support his family after his father's health began to fail. "Anytime you get a chance to represent your country, it's a real honour, but Dad was sick, and under the circumstances, I knew I was doing the right thing," he said.

In August 1979, he signed with the St Louis Blues, and they assigned him to their Central Hockey League (CHL) affiliate, the Salt Lake Golden Eagles. There, he scored 49 goals and 72 points and was voted "Rookie of the Year."

He was recalled to the Blues in 1981 and remained there, amassing an impressive tally of goals and points before being traded to the Calgary Flames. He had been disappointed to move until he experienced an overwhelming welcome from the fans; they were delighted with their new tough goal scorer, and he certainly delivered for them; he consistently performed, scoring 40 goals in five consecutive seasons and, in 1989, lifted the Stanley Cup.

He moved to the Pittsburgh Penguins in 1990; this time, it was Joe's decision. He wanted to raise his family nearer to his hometown and, in 1995, scored his 1000th point. The following year, he signed a one-year contract with the Boston Bruins where he wore number eleven since his usual number seven had been retired in honor of Phil Esposito.

Joe rejoined the Penguins in 1996, and that season, he scored his 500th goal before announcing his retirement. Since then, he has made a new career in coaching.

Although he made hockey history as the first American-born player to score 1000 points in the NHL, he is remarkably humble; "I just consider myself lucky and fortunate. I had the opportunity to play. I worked hard for it, but everything fell into place for me."

11

THE LOCKOUT OF 2004

NHL hockey is not just a game. It is a billion-dollar industry. Every season, behind the scenes, there is a frantic battle to achieve the delicate balance that will satisfy the needs of the executives responsible for the NHL, the managers of the individual franchises, the players, and the fans. As the game has evolved, some changes have caused disputes that have not been easy to resolve.

In the 1924-25 season, for example, the Hamilton Tigers players based in Ontario demanded a pay raise when the number of games they were expected to play was increased from twenty-four to thirty. The franchise argued that the players had no case because they were under contract to play over a specified period, and the number of games within those dates was immaterial. The players were not satisfied and refused to play before the playoffs. As a result, the franchise was dissolved, and the player's contracts were sold.

In 1992, a ten-day strike almost ruined the playoffs when the NHL tried to introduce a salary cap, which would have limited the amount of money teams could spend on their players. Many franchises were paying more than three-quarters of their income on their player's salaries and faced an uncertain future if the situation continued. The NHLPA (NHL Players Association), responsible for looking after players' interests, would not agree to this and called its members to withdraw their labour.

It was a difficult time for many who relied on hockey for their incomes; hotels, sports bars, and souvenir stand owners nervously realized how dependent they were on these negotiations. Big sponsors wondered whether it was worth continuing their investments, and sports television companies faced losing a great deal of revenue. When the strike was resolved - with the issue of the salary cap not solved but put aside for the future - everyone breathed an uneasy sigh of relief.

This issue of the salary cap would not go away, and with no easy solution, the NHL and the NHL Players Association continued to lock horns, each side unable to give way. In 2004, it finally came to a head with several teams on the brink of bankruptcy, and when it became clear that this impasse could not be resolved, on 16 September 2004, what should have been the 88th NHL season was cancelled.

While the arenas remained empty, the men in suits continued to hold talks, both sides desperate to find a long-term, workable solution that would suit all parties. Gary Bettman, NHL Commissioner at the time, believed that he had to stand firm to save the game and stop the inequality that had developed between the richest teams, able to buy star players, and those that were struggling financially, unable to afford top quality players, that gave them little hope of winning support, extra funding and sponsorship.

For the entire season, players, referees and other staff were left without salaries, and many supporters felt bitter. The sport they followed so devotedly, often planning their lives around their team's games, had just stopped.

A lot of people found it difficult to be very sympathetic to the players since their salaries were (and are) undeniably huge. Furthermore, many of the bigger names are offered endorsements, which pay them hundreds of thousands of dollars. However, the NHL players are still poor compared to elite football, baseball and basketball players. Plus, being an athlete in a full-contact sport like hockey comes with risk; careers can be shortened by injuries that, on occasion, can affect the player's quality of life and well-being afterwards. The expectations on the young men who commit to play in the NHL are often difficult - when everything is going well, they are adored - but when they are perceived to have failed, they are vilified. They wanted to play - missing a season could badly affect their game.

Some of the players went to other leagues in Europe and North America at that time, and it has been argued that having some of this NHL top-tier talent did improve and enhance the game in those leagues. Rick Nash of the Columbus Blue Jackets and "Jumbo" Joe Thornton went to play for HC Davos of the Swiss National League A. There, they won the prestigious Spengler Cup and formed a close relationship with the team and returned to Switzerland each summer afterwards for a spell of European training. Henrik Zetterberg, then with the Detroit Red Wings, returned to his native Sweden and played for Times IK of the Swedish Elite League and enjoyed a successful season there, scoring 50 points, before returning to Detroit. Carolina Hurricanes left winger Erik Cole had a great season with Eisbaren Berlin in the DEL (Deutsche Eishockey Liga), and Vincent "Vinny" Lecavalier and his Tampa Bay Lightning teammates, Nikolai Khabibulin and Brad Richards played for Ak Bars Kazan in the Russian Superleague.

Jason Spezza, reluctant to take a break from his fledgling career, left the Ottawa Senators for a season with the Binghamton Senators in the American Hockey League (AHL), and Los Angeles Kings left winger Michael Cammalleri played in the same league, with the Manchester Monarchs.

The lockout lasted for 310 days. A CBA (Collective Bargaining Agreement) was finally reached on 13 July 2005, and the NHL team owners and the NHL Players Association ratified the deal on 22 July.

At the time, a lot of people thought NHL hockey would never recover from the lockout and the fans would never return as they had before. This has not been the case, and after the cap was introduced, the balance between teams has improved, which has made for more exciting and unpredictable games.

Many worry that the lessons of the past have not been learned, however. Industrial action interrupted the 2912-13 season, but after intense negotiations, a ten-year deal was agreed. It is to be hoped that through communication and accepting one another's point of view, the players and the NHL teams will never find themselves in a lockout predicament again, and the Stanley Cup will never be engraved with the words "Season not played" again.

12

THE FINNISH FIGHTER

Saku Koivu was used to fighting determinedly for his team, Montreal Canadien, on the ice and battling against injuries to regain his fitness to play, but nothing could have prepared him for the devastating news he received on 6 September 2001.

Saku was born in Turku, Finland, in 1974 and had grown up in a hockey-playing family. At age twenty-one, he moved overseas to join the Montreal Canadiens (after a season with TPS in the Finnish SM-Liga) and looked forward to a long and successful professional career playing the sport he loved at the highest level.

He quickly proved himself and ranked fourth among the 1993- 94 season rookies with 45 points in 85 games. He missed almost half the following season due to a knee injury but recorded an impressive 56 points in 50 games.

He struggled with more injuries over the next two seasons but proved his resilience and strength to return to the ice and, in 1999, was made the first European captain of his team.

In 2001, after recovering from surgery to his left knee and missing 28 games, he returned to form and finished the season with 47 points. He was looking forward to the next season, captaining the Canadiens to what he hoped would be a successful Stanley Cup run.

Saku was travelling back from a visit to Finland in September 2001 with his teammate, Brian Savage, when he began to feel really sick with serious stomach pains. Brian was concerned about how ill and pale he looked, so as soon as they were back in Montreal, Saku went to see the team physician, who began to run some tests.

The results were devastating. Saku was suffering from Burkitt's lymphoma, non-Hodgkin lymphoma.

Despite being team captain of one of the biggest teams in the NHL, Saku had never courted publicity and had endeavoured to keep his family life very private, but this proved impossible as he began his treatment and news of his cancer soon broke.

Messages of love and support poured in from fans and supporters of the game, and Saku was particularly grateful when Pittsburgh Penguins Mario Lemieux, the

"Magnificent One," who had recovered from Hodgkin's lymphoma in 1997, and retired Tampa Bay Lightning center, John Cullen, who had also recovered from cancer, offered their encouragement and advice.

He endured chemotherapy and radiotherapy treatments and was expected to miss the entire 2001-02 season, but he made a remarkable recovery - and made his comeback just in time for the last few games.

When he returned to the ice on 9 April 2002, the 80th game of the season, the fans cheered in delight and gave him a standing ovation that lasted eight minutes. Their captain was back!

After the 2002 playoffs, he was awarded the Bill Masterson Memorial Trophy. It was given to him in recognition of his courage in the face of such a gravely serious disease, but also his leadership and commitment to his team even while he was undergoing treatment.

Having made a recovery, Saku was determined to make a difference for others suffering from cancer and launched the Saku Koivu Foundation, which raises funds for cancer research, particularly for Montreal General Hospital, and supports projects to improve the lives of young people undergoing treatment.

He also wanted to resume his career. He trained hard and focused on his game, and the 2002- 03 season was his best to date, having scored 71 points (21 goals and

50 assists). The following season, he was disappointed to miss thirteen games with a knee injury, and, in the 2004 -05 Lockout, he returned to his old team in Finland, where his father was head coach.

Back in Canada, for the 2005- 06 season, Saku suffered a very serious injury to his left eye in a game against the Carolina Hurricanes on 26 April. He underwent surgery for a detached retina but lost some of his peripheral vision and needed further eye surgery afterwards. Since then, he has worn a larger visor for protection and has had to accept he might never regain his full vision.

Saku reached 500 points in January 2007, and in October 2008, he reached his 600th career point. The following year, he left the Canadiens after ten years and signed with the Anaheim Ducks, where he remained until announcing his retirement on 10 September 2014.

Saku also had a distinguished international career as captain of the Finnish team and won an Olympic silver medal at the 2006 Turin Games and Olympic bronze at the 1994 Lillehammer Games, the 1998 Nagano Games and the 2010 Vancouver Games.

Saku has become an inspiration to many, not just athletes, with his positive and tenacious approach to life and his courage in overcoming the terrible disease that is cancer. He said, in an interview in March 2012, just before his 1000th NHL game, "During my cancer treatments, I never thought about what would happen with hockey. It was more important just to survive and beat the disease. Since then, I'm allowing myself to enjoy life and hockey more.... I feel I've accomplished a lot, and I'm okay with that."

13

REALIZING A DREAM

There is a well-used expression, 'Good things come to those that wait,' but sometimes, it becomes necessary to stop waiting and take action to make your own luck, and this is something Raymond Jean Bourque knows all about.

He was born in the small town of Saint-Laurent, Quebec in 1960. His father was a hockey enthusiast, so Ray started on the ice at an early age and played on frozen ponds and local ice rinks. From the start, he demonstrated an impressive dedication to the sport and spent hours at a time practicing and developing his skills. His parents always taught him the value of hard work and humility, values that he carried with him throughout his long career.

As a junior, he played with Soreland Verdun in the Quebec Major Junior Hockey League, then started his college career at the University of New Brunswick. There, he quickly became known as a defenseman of great quality, with the rare ability to make an offensive contribution for his team.

In the 1979 NHL Entry Draft, the Boston Bruins selected him with the eighth overall pick, and he soon proved his worth when he scored a goal in his first game against the Winnipeg Jets.

It was the start of an enviable relationship between a star player and a team. Ray proved himself time and time again with his outstanding playmaking skills, and the fans loved him. In his first seasons, he was given the Number 7 jersey, which had previously been the legendary Phil Esposito's. In 1987, after Espo's induction into the Hockey Hall of Fame, the Bruins decided to honour him by retiring his jersey. At that ceremony, Ray wore two jerseys and skating onto the ice, he took off the first number 7 jersey and handed it reverently to the old master whilst at the same time revealing his own new number, 77, and he would wear that number for the remainder of his career.

As captain for fifteen seasons, Ray was determined to bring Boston a championship, and no one doubted his commitment to winning the Stanley Cup. Season after season, the team battled for the trophy and came tantalizingly close, reaching the finals against the Edmonton Oilers in 1988 and again in 1990. "I don't like losing... Being a competitive player, it's not a good feeling." Ray said in an interview.

It wasn't just Ray's prowess on the ice that so endeared him to the public; he was always willing to continue playing for the Bruins without putting the franchise through lengthy and difficult negotiations. This loyalty, whilst appreciated by the fans, was not very helpful for the NHL Players Association, who were desperately trying to negotiate and increase players' salaries.

The Bruins 1999- 00 season was beset by injuries, and they failed to qualify for the 2000 Stanley Cup playoffs. Ray was well aware his long NHL career was coming to an end, and he really wanted to have his name engraved on the Cup before he retired. If he couldn't achieve this with his beloved Bruins, he would have to look elsewhere.

In 2000, he swapped his black and gold Bruins jersey for the burgundy, silver and steel blue of the Colorado Avalanche and a chance of lifting the Stanley Cup. In 2001, after he had played 1,612 regular season games and 214 playoff games, his dream finally came true.

To celebrate his win, he took the Cup to a rally at Boston's City Hall Plaza, where some 20,000 fans cheered for him. After all, he had always said he would bring it to Boston, though it was bittersweet that he hadn't done it with the Bruins. Shortly afterwards, he announced his retirement. In his long career, he scored 410 goals, 1169 assists and attained 1579 points!

He had won nine James Norris Memorial Trophies. He had played for the NHL All-Stars in Rendez-Vous '87 against the Soviet Union - and, internationally, he played for Team Canada in 1981, 1984 and 1987

Canada Cup and reached the semi-finals in the 1998 Nagano Winter Olympic Games.

Ray remains one of the Boston Bruins' all-time greats. Following his induction into the Hockey Hall of Fame in 2004 (which was the first year he was eligible), both the Boston Bruins and Colorado Avalanche retired his number 77 shirt, an honour they have only given to a handful of players.

14

THE GREAT ONE

Statistically, Wayne Gretsky is, without a doubt, the greatest hockey player of all time. He holds, or shares, sixty NHL records, including the most goals of all time (894) and in a season (215), the most points in a career (2,857) and the most hat tricks in a regular season (50). Despite all this, he does not believe he is a naturally gifted player.

He was born in Branford, Ontario, in 1961, and he started skating as a two-year-old at his grandparents' farm and then, back in Brantford, on a rink his father had made in their backyard. He, his three brothers, and their little sister learned to play, skating around obstacles and flipping pucks over them.

Wayne demonstrated a rare ability and, at the age of six, began playing with the Brantford Nadrofsky Steelers in a team of ten-year-olds. As his team jersey was far too large for him, he had to tuck it into the right side of his pants, and he continued to do this, for luck, throughout his playing career.

By the time he was ten, Wayne had scored 378 goals and 139 assists in one season - an astonishing tally that attracted some attention from the local press. In the 1974 Quebec International Pee-Wee Hockey Tournament, he scored 26 goals, and by the age of thirteen, he had scored more than 1,000 goals!

Unfortunately, with all of this success came jealousy and bad feelings. Some of the parents of the other boys on his team were unhappy that their children were being overlooked when Wayne, the child prodigy, was on the ice and loudly accused him of "hogging the puck." Wayne found this criticism hard to bear, and when they booed and jeered at him as he played, he even considered quitting hockey.

Growing up, hockey was not his only love. Wayne has frequently mentioned his passion for baseball, and, as a kid, he was a huge Detroit Tigers fan, so it is just possible that had he decided to hang up his skates, he might well have blazed a trail in a completely different sport.

Concerned about their son's well-being, Wayne's parents arranged for him to play in Toronto instead. This was not straightforward as there were strict rules in place, and they were forced to make a legal challenge to the Canadian Amateur Hockey Association so that their son could play outside their home area. After gaining permission, Wayne played in the junior hockey league with the Toronto Nationals.

These difficulties do not seem to have had a long-term detrimental effect on Wayne since he has spoken about children enjoying sports, saying, "The only way a kid is going to practice is if it's total fun for him... and it was for me."

At the age of sixteen, Wayne was selected by the Sault Ste. Marie Greyhounds. His parents arranged for him to stay with family friends in northern Ontario, and it was there that he first started wearing his famous number 99 jersey (he had originally wanted to wear number 9, like his hockey hero Gordie Howe, but that jersey had already been taken).

At that time, NHL teams could not offer contracts to players under the age of twenty, so, in 1978, the Indianapolis Racers, a WHA (World Hockey Association), offered Wayne, then aged seventeen, a contract worth US $1,75 million, and he signed. It soon became clear, however, that the Racers were in serious financial difficulties, and after having played just eight games, Wayne was traded to the Edmonton Oilers.

In his first NHL season (1979- 80), Wayne tied with Marcel Dionne for most points (137) and was awarded the Hart Memorial Trophy for the most valuable NHL player - which was the first of his eight consecutive Hart awards!

As center and team captain, Wayne led the Oilers to four Stanley Cup victories (in 1984, 1985, 1987, and 1988). After the 1987- 88 season, he was traded to the Los Angeles Kings.

Early in the 1989- 90 season, he broke Gordie Howe's NHL scoring record of 1,850 points and then, in the 1993- 94 season, he broke his hero's record for career goals when he recorded his 801st.

In 1996, Wayne was traded again, this time to the St Louis Blues, and then he signed with the New York Rangers. There, in 1997, he broke another record with his 1,851st assist. He retired after the 1998- 99 season and, as one of many tributes, the NHL retired his Number 99 jersey.

But Wayne was not just a scoring machine; his style of play had a strong influence on his teams, and after their successes, other teams adopted similar strategies. He maintains that ninety percent of his game is mental and has an instinctive awareness of the positions of his teammates throughout a game. With this map in his head, he also had the ability to anticipate play from the opposing team, and it was this more cerebral approach that made his contribution so exciting. "I just get a feeling about where a teammate is going to be. A lot of the time, I can turn and pass without even looking."

Wayne believes that he had to rely on using his vision and his mental abilities in his game while he was a youngster, playing against boys much bigger and stronger than he was. "I wasn't naturally gifted with regard to size or speed..." he has said. He also maintains that he is not a particularly competitive person.

Many of his fans don't altogether agree with his view of his hockey skills; they have watched in awe as entire teams converged on him, only to find that he had already slipped the puck to a teammate; they marvelled at his clinical accuracy, firing goal after goal on target, and became accustomed to seeing him move across the ice with such purpose and grace, rarely breathing hard, even after more than twenty minutes of play, and making it all look so easy.

They firmly believe that he played hockey like no one had ever been able to manage before and find it hard to imagine they will ever see him like that again.

15

A LITTLE KNOWN STORY

When Jon Cooper, head coach of the Tampa Bay Lightning, was asked about some of the most impressive performances he had seen from players in his long association with hockey, he recounted a little-known story about a young Canadian goaltender who demonstrated extraordinary resilience and recovery after a very traumatic experience. He was thinking about Dustin Tokarski.

"Ticker," as Dustin was known to his teammates, was playing for the Syracuse Crunch, the Tampa Bay Lightning's AHL (American Hockey League) team at the time.

In October 2012, when he was twenty-three, Ticker was carjacked at knifepoint. Being the victim of such a potentially violent and frightening crime is difficult for the biggest, strongest members of society, and afterwards, Ticker found himself reporting the crime at a Syracuse police station when he should have been preparing himself for a road game against the Binghamton Senators, scheduled for that very day.

After he had made his statement to the police and worked through the necessary paperwork with the police officers, they sent him on his way with their best wishes - and fervent hopes for a win for their local team.

After a dash to the Brooke Veterans Memorial Arena in New York, Ticker arrived at the nick of time, just as the national anthem was being played. His team and the Crunch staff were aware of what he had been through and had no intention of expecting him to play.

Unfortunately, it soon became clear this was to be a bad-tempered game, and the Crunch was 5-0 behind by the second period when their Finnish goaltender, Riku Helenius, raced over to his opposite number, Robin Lehner, with his fists flying.

This line brawl resulted in both goalies being ejected from the game, and exasperated, the coach turned to Ticker.

The young goalie skated onto the crease, with his team expecting little from him; after all, it had only been a couple of hours since he had faced a knifeman. But the Crunch suddenly made an extraordinary fight back and scored goal after goal while Ticker prevented fourteen shots from entering his nets.

By the end of the game, the two teams had drawn level, 5-5, and, in overtime, it was the Crunch that scored the deciding goal. Victory!

"That was one of the biggest comebacks I've ever been a part of," recalled Jon Cooper. "That's just Ticker - he somehow finds a way."

16

KEEPING THE FAITH

Throughout our lives, it is important to try to keep our priorities and hold onto the values and ethics that are important to us. Pressures, demands and distractions on our time and attention can make this difficult, and although top athletes appear to have an enviable lifestyle with great wealth and privilege, these young men and women are just as vulnerable to mental health issues, poor decisions and a lack of definition to their lives.

Mike Fisher, Ottawa Senators and Nashville Predators center, knows the importance of having a strong faith as the bedrock for his life.

He was born in June 1980 in Peterborough, Ontario and was raised in a happy, Christian household, regularly attending church services and following Jesus; his uncle is a former chaplain to the Toronto Blue Jays baseball club.

When he started playing hockey at the age of seven, some of the other children teased him about his faith, and because of his Christianity, the expectation seemed to be that he would lack the aggression required to excel at hockey, but this was definitely not the case.

Mike wanted to play hard. He looked up to tough NHL players that he knew were Christians: Detroit Red Wings and Toronto Maple Leafs left wing Mark Osborne and center Dean McAmmond, who had played in several NHL franchises, but he particularly admired the "Grim Reaper," the no-nonsense, fearsome enforcer, Stu Grimson. Stu, known for being well-read and intelligent, was a born-again Christian and led the NHL's Christian Fellowship.

After developing his talent in the OHA (Ontario Hockey Association) Junior Peterborough Petes and the Sudbury Wolves, he was drafted by the Ottawa Senators in the 2nd round of the 1998 Draft.

Unfortunately, Mike's first season was interrupted by injury, and he was only able to record 9 points in his 32 games. In the seasons that followed, however, he gained quite a reputation as a hard man, and in his fourth season with the Senators, he scored 18 goals and 38 points.

As a young NHL star, away from the steadying influence of his family, Mike was not content, spiritually. He had been so focused on hockey that he had forgotten that his soul and his faith needed nourishing, and, with a great deal of money and the company of people who did not have the same core of faith that he had, Mike was making some bad decisions.

Mike was living with his cousin, Warren Robinson and his wife in Almonte, and they found it very difficult to see how Mike was losing his way. Warren invited him to a Bible study meeting, and as Mike began to really listen to God's word as they read the verses, he realized how much he had neglected his faith and felt ashamed.

From then on, he made a promise to dedicate his life to Jesus and vowed to glory God with the special gift - for hockey - he had been given.

To help him remain focussed on what is important to him while on the ice, Mike always has a verse from the Bible, Romans 12:12, from one of Paul's letters to the Romans, written on his hockey stick, underneath the rubber grip. It says, "Be joyful in hope, patient in affliction, faithful in prayer," words that have always resonated with him.

During the Lock Out season of 2004- 05, he played in Europe for EV Zug in the Swiss Nationalliga A, and then, back in Ottawa, his form continued to improve. He signed another five-year contract with the Senators in 2007, and in the season that followed, he scored his career-best 23 goals!

In February 2011, Mike was traded to the Nashville Predators. He had married the country music singer (and American Idol winner) Carrie Underwood, and this move now suited both of the couple's careers.

In 2012, Mike was handed the NHL Foundation Player Award for the player who most "applies the core values of hockey (commitment, perseverance and teamwork) to enrich the lives of others in the community," in recognition of his outstanding charitable work.

Mike remained with the Predators and, in 2016, was named captain of the team. He attacked the role with determination and drive and led them to the 2017 Stanley Cup Finals - but were ultimately beaten by the Pittsburgh Penguins.

The following year, Mike announced his retirement but, in 2018, couldn't resist coming out of retirement to join his old team for a final Stanley Cup run, but it wasn't to be (they were eliminated in the second round), and Mike retired for a second time.

Since ending his NHL career, Mike has dedicated himself to helping and mentoring young people, with an emphasis on hockey, but more importantly, faith. He actively supports camps organized by Hockey Ministries International in his hometown, Peterborough, as well as in Ottawa. He also enjoys hunting, a pastime he always enjoyed with his father and extended family, growing up. He has explained that, although some people don't understand, he enjoys the comradeship rather than the killing, and it gives him time for quiet reflection.

Mike hopes that he can help children learn to be bold about their beliefs and not be frightened to speak out about them. In his book *Defender of the Faith*, he wrote,

"It's something to be definitely proud of, and be able to share it. Whatever God's gifted you with, put the Lord at the centre of it. And there's no way to peace and happiness like the Lord can bring. And it's exciting because it's free. You don't have to go out and earn it. You just got to accept it."

17

PLAYFUL PRANKS

Tricks and pranks are embedded into the psyche of hockey players, just as it is in other team sports. Athletes who work hard often like to play hard as a release. So, planning elaborate jokes on teammates is a great way for them to bond together. It has also become an accepted way for veteran players to bring cocky rookies down a peg or two - or help younger players quickly lose some of their inhibitions, get over their nerves and become a part of the 'family.'

When Brandon Duhaime joined the Minnesota Wild franchise in 2019, he found his car had been completely crammed full of styrofoam packing peanuts by his new teammates while he was practicing on the ice. Tom Wilson, having joined the Washington Capitals, was treated to a more public caper when serial prankster Alex Ovechkin managed to 'pie' him in the face with a plate of shaving cream - in front of an arena of players, spectators, management and reporters.

Goaltender Marc-André Fleury gained quite a reputation as a master prankster in his long NHL career. Soon after Justin Schultz was traded to his team, the Pittsburgh Penguins, he returned from practice to find the goalie had hung all of his street clothes from the rafters of the building. Mr. Fleury, also known as "Flowers," has also removed every item of furniture, luggage and kit from a teammate's hotel room and into the hall, zipped himself inside a hockey bag to scare Colby Armstrong half to death, and tightly rolled up all of Kris Letang's possessions into a ball and then covered it with tape.

It isn't just the players who like to play tricks. In 2017, the Tampa Bay Lightning management called a meeting to unveil their 'new' jersey to those expected to wear it - a riot of palm trees and stripes, a world away from the simple and classy blue and white design the players were expecting. It was, of course, a joke! Ha!

Philadelphia Flyers equipment manager Derek Settlemyre was able to get hold of an extremely lifelike rubber cobra and attached it to the lid of one of the Gatorade coolers so it popped up when the players went to get a drink. Poor Luke Schen did not enjoy the experience, snakes being his "worst fear in the world," and Michael Raffl dropped his stick and fled when he went to get a drink. In fact, it was only cool-as-a-cucumber defenseman Michael Del Zotto who was not taken in by the fake snake. Afterwards, Derek confessed that it had been veteran Green Bay Packers equipment manager Gordon "Red" Batty who had put him up to it; he had played the same trick on another team many years before.

The award for the most elaborate prank, however, surely must go to one of NHL's most colourful personalities, center Jeremy Roenick.

While JR was signed to the San Jose Sharks, he was enjoying an offseason break in Las Vegas with two younger players, Torrey Mitchell, who was 23 at the time, and Devin Setoguchi, aged 21. One evening, the three were playing cards at a casino when a mysterious stranger introduced himself and invited them to a very exclusive, black-tie party later that night.

This party was at a mansion, and after a limousine ride from their hotel, they arrived and gave the password the stranger had given them before they could enter. As soon as they went inside, Mitchy began to feel apprehensive; he thought there was something peculiar about the other guests. JR agreed but suggested they should stay for a while before they made their excuses so as not to cause offence.

They were directed into a large room where they could hear eerie music, and around thirty people were there, speaking in low voices, and gave the three NHL players the impression that they were not altogether welcome there.

A waitress brought them shot glasses filled with what appeared to be blood, and then a very attractive young woman wearing only her underwear was introduced to the company as "the main event." After she had greeted everybody, she left the room.

By then, Mitchy was wondering what on earth they had stumbled into and thought perhaps something really sinister was going on. Their fears were confirmed when the woman they had just met was wheeled back into the room on a hospital bed, and when the sheet that covered her was removed, she appeared to have been "filleted from the neck down to the waist" with some of her 'organs' plainly on view. He stole a look at the other guests and saw that they now all had fangs and red, glowing eyes.

Horrified, Mitchy turned to JR, who was already running for the door, shouting. Worse was to come - a guard at the door quickly moved towards him, and, as JR begged for mercy, the bouncer 'stabbed' him repeatedly, with blood flying everywhere.

That was enough for Mitchy. Looking around, he saw a window and ran at it, breaking through the glass and landing on the grass below. As soon as he was on his feet, he ran (with all of his athletic training) as far as his legs could carry him.

As he ran, his mobile phone rang repeatedly, but there was no way he was going to stop until he was well away from that horrible place.

Eventually, he came to a stop and answered his phone. To his astonishment (and relief), it was JR, helpless with laughter, telling him to come back; he was alive and well and that it had all been a prank.

JR had gone to extraordinary lengths to pull off what he called "the best prank ever in the history of the NHL." He had hired the mansion a whole cast of actors and proved himself to be quite the thespian in the process.

It is said that the whole escapade was filmed that night, but few have seen it - it is thought that the Sharks management who, while privately entertained by these high jinks, very sensibly had no interest in creating any distractions from the important business of hockey and winning on the ice.

18

SHARPSHOOTER

Paul Kariya was born in North Vancouver, British Columbia, in 1974. His father, a Japanese-Canadian who had been born in an internment camp in the Second World War, had played rugby with the Canadian national team, and his mother was also an athlete. Paul, his three brothers, and his sister were encouraged to try all sports, and they were a highly competitive household.

After learning to figure skate, Paul and his brothers, Steve and Martin, naturally gravitated towards hockey. Paul has spoken of enjoying 'free ice' at 05h30 every Sunday morning at his local Karen Magnussen arena, where he worked on his skating skills before practising smashing shots at targets he had marked on a shed in his backyard - until it could barely stand.

As a teenager, he built his strength by taking construction work in the summer and, no doubt, this gave him an understanding of teamwork and maturity that would be a great asset to his play.

Paul left home at sixteen to play Junior A hockey in Penticton for two seasons (and recorded 45 goals and 112 points in 54 games in his 1st season, then 46 goals and 132 points over 40 games in the 2nd, marking him out as a potential future superstar). At eighteen, he received offers from Boston University and Harvard University but enrolled at the University of Maine and joined the Maine Black Bears.

His college playing career was just as successful; he was awarded Hockey East's Rookie and Player of the Year and, in 1993, the Hobey Baker Award as the National Collegiate Athletics Association's (NCAA) top player.

Paul was selected in the Mighty Ducks of Anaheim's first-ever NHL Entry Draft pick in 1993, then returned to his sophomore year at Maine as captain of the Black Bears until that December, when he was committed to the Canadian national team for the 1994 Winter Olympics.

After winning an Olympic silver medal at Lillehammer, Norway, he decided not to return to Maine but to turn professional with the Mighty Ducks.

Due to the NHL lockout, Paul's NHL debut was delayed until January 1995, but from then on, he was a class act! Commentators tentatively compared him with Wayne Gretzky and wondered whether hockey had found his natural successor, and 'The Greatest' himself was just as admiring of the young player's exciting play and superb skills.

Game 6 of the Stanley Cup finals in 2003, in which the Mighty Ducks faced the New Jersey Devils, would have a lasting effect on Paul and eventually on hockey itself. Paul found himself up against Scott Stevens, one of the NHL's greatest open-ice-hitters of all time. Known as "Captain Crunch," he had a formidable reputation as a ferocious adversary.

With his team down, Paul was passing the puck to a teammate and did not see Captain Crunch coming. The defenseman brutally dropped him with his shoulder. Paul fell to the ice, on his back, and remained there motionless for 48 seconds.

The arena watched, open-mouthed in horror, hardly daring to look away in what seemed an age before Paul started to move. His eyes opened, and after gazing at the bright lights, he took a deep breath that clouded his visor. He managed to stagger to his feet, and his teammates helped him from the ice. He was taken to the dressing room but quickly returned to the bench, and minutes later, he was allowed to return to the ice.

In an astonishing about-turn, Paul suddenly fired a stinging slip shot past the Devils' goaltender, and the Ducks eventually won the game 5-2. Sadly, for Anaheim, it would not be the fairytale ending they had hoped for, and the Ducks ultimately lost in Game 7.

After the game, the Duck management found little to complain about. They considered Scott Stevens a fair (yet tough) player and agreed with the NHL director of officiating that he had made a clean hit on their captain. However, in the weeks that followed, Paul had absolutely no recollection of the game, the hit, his goal, or anything whatsoever from that game.

Paul's career continued, and, in his 15-season career, he later played with the Colorado Avalanche, the Nashville Predators and the St Louis Blues. Although he was a fine player by any standard, he never quite regained the promise he had shown before the incident with Captain Crush, and he was blighted by injury. Nevertheless, he recorded 989 points in 989 regular season games and won two NHL Lady Byng Trophies. His Japanese ancestry made him a firm favourite with East Asian NHL fans at a time when the sport was gaining popularity, especially in Japan.

After suffering from six concussions and sitting out most of the 2010-11 season due to post-concussion syndrome, Paul had had enough. His brain function had decreased significantly in tests, and he announced his retirement on 29 June 2011, aged thirty-four.

When he was inducted into the Hockey Hall of Fame in 2017, he had made a good recovery but mentioned in his speech that his cognitive skills were not always as they had been. He did not speak about his head injuries, preferring to concentrate on the award of, he said, "the greatest honour I could have imagined."

A private and quiet person, he had no desire to become a big voice for changes in hockey since he was satisfied with the precautions and protective measures the NHL had introduced, although he has concerns that targeted head shots are still part of the game.

Since then, Paul has taken on the new challenge of surfing. He tellingly calls it a "peaceful sport," and he also enjoys yoga. He tends to look forward and doesn't dwell on his past career very much, but sometimes he wishes he was remembered for his play on the ice rather than being out cold and for a goal he still can't bring to mind. "... there were tough times for sure, but the great times far outweigh those," he has said.

19

'BOOMER' BAUN

When Bobby Baun passed away on 14 August 2023, aged eighty-six, the Maple Leafs lost one of their greatest characters and best-loved players. In his later years, he liked nothing more than reminiscing about his career in the NHL, giving younger fans a colourful and fascinating insight into hockey in the middle part of the 20th Century.

Bobby, or 'Boomer,' was born in September 1936 in Lanigan, Saskatchewan, but his family moved to Toronto when he was three. He started playing junior hockey with the Toronto Marlboros (of the Ontario Hockey Association) in 1952 and won the Memorial Cup with them in 1955 and 1956.

He left school in 10th grade to become a professional and signed with the Toronto Maple Leafs. In his first season (1956- 57), he started in their affiliate team in the American Hockey League, the Rochester Americans, but was soon called up to the Leafs, and there he remained for the next eleven seasons.

Boomer won the Stanley Cup with the Leafs in 1962, 1963, 1964 and 1967, and though all of these victories were undoubtedly sweet, it was his performance in the 1964 playoffs that has gone down famously in NHL history.

The Maple Leafs were battling the Detroit Red Wings for the Cup, and, in Game 6, they were trailing 3 - 2 when Boomer (who had been in the penalty box for two of the Wings' goals) had blocked a sharp shot from Gordie Howe to prevent a penalty.

He felt something snap in his ankle, and when he tried to get up, he found he couldn't put any weight on it. With 13:15 remaining in the third period, he was stretchered off. He wasn't sure what he had done but imagined it was probably a pinched nerve; it just felt numb.

The team medics had a quick look at it, and Boomer asked if he could do further damage if he continued to play. When they said they didn't think so, he asked them to give him something to freeze it, and then they strapped it up so he could re-enter the fray.

And what a return he made! With the scores level as the game went into overtime, Boomer managed to negotiate a winning shot from the right that soared past the Detroit goalie, Terry Sawchuk, and secured a Maple Leaf victory.

Afterwards, Boomer described his effort as a "triple-flutter- blast with a follow-up blooper" and, in his 2000 biography Lowering the Boom, admitted he would always be grateful for "the Goal."

Two nights later, it was Game 7. Boomer could barely walk and relied on having his ankle joint frozen and Novocain painkilling injections every ten minutes throughout the game in order to see him through. His teammate, Red Kelly, had torn ligaments in the same game that Boomer had picked up his injury, and he needed the same treatment. Finally, the Leafs won 4 - 0 and lifted the Stanley Cup once more. "Was it worth it? Sure it was. That's how much winning the Stanley Cup meant to me. Most hockey players would tell you they'd do the very same thing", Boomer mused years later.

It soon became apparent that Boomer's injury was more serious than he had realized, and once he had had an X-ray, medical staff confirmed it was fractured, and his leg was encased in a cast while it healed. After six weeks, however, Boomer had had enough of that and soaked it off in his bathtub.

"The more positive thoughts we can put in our heads, the better we're going to be. That's exactly what I'm like in everything. You can't get through life with a negative attitude."

This wasn't the only time he had endured serious injury while playing; on another occasion, he had received a skate cut to his neck that had started to hemorrhage while he was outside after the game, waiting to get on the team bus. His fellow defenseman, Tim Horton, found him and carried him to the nearest hospital. Once he had been given several pints of blood by transfusion, Boomer found himself in a hospital bed next to his wife, who was in the process of giving birth to their third son.

He also maintained that he played for five years with a broken neck that he knew nothing about and put it down to having a naturally high pain threshold.

Boomer finally parted company with the Maple Leafs for the Oakland Seals in the 1967 Expansion Draft, but after limited play due to a broken toe, he joined the Detroit Red Wings. As a professional with twelve seasons behind him, he had developed an understanding of the business side of the game and encouraged players to fight for better pay. He told Gordy Howe that he should ask for a raise, particularly since he was being paid a good deal more than the Red Wings legend and when Gordy put this to the franchise management, they agreed and paid him what he asked. In the days before a players union, and with much less money in the game (when Boomer started in the NHL, some players had to support themselves with second jobs), players were grateful for his advice.

In 1970, Boomer returned to Toronto, and he remained there until 1972, when he injured his neck, and his doctors told him, in no uncertain terms, that he risked serious damage to his health and mobility if he continued playing.

He finished his career with 37 goals - an impressive tally for a man who always said that his job was to stop goals and not to score them, 224 points and 1,489 penalty minutes in 964 regular season games and another 3 goals, and 171 penalty minutes in 96 playoff games. He had a well-earned reputation as a tough, resilient hard-man on the ice and one of the hardest hitters of his time.

But there was more to Boomer. As a young player, he had been very impressed by One of his contemporaries, Bobby Hull, "the Golden Jet," whom he saw signing autographs to a large group of fans crowding around him. He did not stop until every single person had received his signature and a friendly word, and Boomer resolved to always do the same.

Although he kept his family life private, he always had time for his supporters and those who had the pleasure of meeting him always remember how charming and generous he was. This was worded perfectly in the NHL Alumni Association's tribute on learning of his death; "his legacy of kindness and compassion will be remembered fondly."

20

INCREDIBLE GENEROSITY

The King Clancy Memorial Trophy is an annual award for the player who best demonstrates leadership qualities on and off the ice and who makes a noteworthy humanitarian contribution to his community.

It was established in 1988 by the NHL Board of Governors to honour the late Frank "King" Clancy, a great philanthropist, social reformer, and legendary player, referee, and coach.

Players nominated for this award feel a special sense of pride and achievement, and none more than PK Subban, who was handed the trophy in 2022.

PK (Pernell-Karl) was born in Toronto on 30 May, 1989. His parents were immigrants from the Caribbean, and they raised their family in the Rexdale neighbourhood, near the school where Karl, PK's father, was the principal. Maria, his mother, worked as a bank officer.

PK has four siblings, and he and his two brothers, Malcolm and Jordan, played junior hockey with the Belleville Bulls in the Ontario Hockey League (OHL).

From an early age, PK was one to watch, and in his final season as a junior, he finished with 76 points in 56 games. He had been drafted by the Montreal Canadiens in the 2007 NHL Entry Draft, and two weeks after his last junior game, he began the 09/10 season with the Hamilton Bulldogs, Montreal's American Hockey League (AHL) affiliate.

Despite being born and raised in Toronto, PK had never been a Maple Leafs fan; he had always wanted to play for the Canadiens. His hockey idol had been Jean Béliveau, so he was delighted to realize this exciting opportunity.

His first season could hardly have been better. He was called up to the Canadiens in February 2010 and recorded his first NHL point in his debut game against the Philadelphia Flyers. He was called up again for the Canadiens Stanley Cup playoffs and scored his first goal in Game 1 of his team's second-round series against the Pittsburgh Penguins. After the Canadiens were eliminated, he was returned to the Hamiltonian, and, at the end of the season, he was named a First Team AHL All-Rookie Team after recording 18 goals, 35 assists and 46 points in 77 games.

In the 2011-12 season, PK played 80 games for the Canadiens and on 20 March 2011, he became their first rookie defenseman to score a hat-trick in an 8-1 victory against the Minnesota Wild. He finished that spectacular season with 7 goals and 29 assists. The following season, he played 42 games, partly due to a labour lockout, but scored 11 goals and 27 assists, recorded 38 points, and was awarded the James Norris Memorial Trophy, which is the trophy that goes to the best defensive player.

PK's hard-hitting style of play excited his fans, and he had become a firm favourite. The franchise recognized his value, and after salary arbitration after the 2013- 14 season, he became the highest-paid defenseman in the NHL. In September 2014, he was named alternate captain (with Max Pacioretty, Tomáš Plekanec and Andrei Markov).

In 2016, PK was traded to the Nashville Predators. In his first season, he recorded 40 points in 60 games and was tantalizingly close to lifting the Stanley Cup, but the Predators fell at the last hurdle, defeated by the Pittsburgh Penguins.

After two seasons, PK was traded again, this time to the New Jersey Devils, and while he was there, he faced his former clubs, the Canadiens and then the Predators, where the fans gave him a standing ovation and a tribute video. But his form was slipping; he recorded 18 points in 68 games, and in September 2022, he knew it was time to hang up his skates.

Since he had started his career as a young man, PK had not been satisfied with simply playing hockey. He had visited Haiti in 2011 with former NHL player Georges Laraque to see the reconstruction of a children's hospital in Port-au-Prince that had been devastated in the 2010 earthquake that killed an estimated 300,000 and left more than a million people homeless. The NHL Players Association was helping to fund the project, and seeing the poverty and disease that had developed because the homeless were being forced to live in large tent camps gave him a different perspective on life. "I've never seen a country like that. I've never seen a city in that state..." he said. "It's definitely a life-changing experience."

PK was also involved in helping to support a young player he met through his old minor hockey coach and family friend, Alex Shapiro. When Alex passed away from cancer at just eleven years of age, PK vowed to do all he could to do something positive. To this end, he started the PK Subban Foundation in 2014 with a mission to build "a community of people who are passionate about helping children around the globe." The foundation has raised millions of dollars for causes close to PK's heart and has overseen hockey camps and tournaments for disadvantaged kids.

The following year, PK went further and pledged $10 million to Montreal Children's Hospital, the largest donation ever made by a Canadian athlete. He really wanted to make a difference after seeing how Alex and his parents had suffered during his cancer battle, and when the hospital handed him the proposal, he said he didn't need to think twice before signing it. When his donation was made public, and the hospital atrium, a large public space at the centre of the hospital's new facilities, was named in his honour, PK met some of the young patients and said, "Montreal has given me so much, and today I want to give back."

While he was in Nashville, he introduced the Blue-Line Buddies program with the Metro Nashville Police Department for underprivileged youths. The idea was to bring them and their families together with law enforcement representatives to help create a better understanding between the police and the poorer parts of the community.

Being a black player in the NHL has, on occasion, been challenging. During the protests following the death of George Floyd in 2020, PK spoke out in praise of the NHL community and its rapid decision to support the Black Lives Matter movement. He also made a personal donation of $50,000 for Gianna, George Floyd's daughter.

PK's brother, Jordan, was playing for South Carolina, an affiliate of the Washington Capitals, when he was subjected to racial abuse by an opponent during a 2022 game. PK remarked, "I'm embarrassed because our game is better than this." He went on to say, "But the unfortunate thing is how many kids deal with this every day..." Even though he has said that he doesn't believe there is a real problem with racism in the NHL, he has said it is important that the sport continues to move forward.

Since retiring, PK has become a hockey analyst with a major sports cable channel and continues his charitable work for the causes he cares about. When he looks back over his career, he does have one regret; "I wanted to win a Stanley Cup, but it's a team sport. You can't do it all." he said.

CONCLUSION

We hope you enjoyed reading these short stories about the greatest and most inspirational players to ever grace the ice.

We wish you the best of luck in your hockey playing (or watching) career!

If you enjoyed reading this book, please feel free to leave a kind review on Amazon - it helps our small business more than you will ever know!

* * *

Be sure to check out the following page to see our next Hockey book for Kids!

ALSO BY HCK PRESS

400+ Fun & Unbelievable Hockey Facts for Kids

Discover Crazy Comebacks, Diligent Defensemen, Silly Superstitions & So Much More! (The Perfect Gift for Hockey Lovers & Young Readers)

Order on Amazon now!

Manufactured by Amazon.ca
Acheson, AB